Collins

Revised Tune In!

Adheres to National Education Policy
PREPARATORY STAGE

Author and Series Editor: Dr K Padmini Shankar

Preface

Revised Tune In! is an innovative listening and speaking course that is closely aligned with the National Education Policy, 2020. The course consists of eight books for Classes 1 to 8 with their accompanying audio-visual resources.

Aims

The main aim of *Revised Tune In*! is to help students gain communicative competence in using English in the real world by developing the key aural and oral skills. It aids to boost confidence in learners to develop fluency in using English in academic, personal and social contexts. It uses a step-by-step interactive approach with experiential tasks based on 21st century skills to help learners listen, understand and respond appropriately.

The number of chapters ranges from 10 to 13 in each level. Each chapter is built around a theme and focuses on specific language and communicative functions related to it. Special focus is also given on enriching the fund of context-specific vocabulary and spoken grammar, along with the use of correct pronunciation, intonation, stress and pause.

The chapters are structured to include the following sections:

Learning objectives defines language learning goals at the beginning of each chapter.

Getting started introduces the theme in an engaging way.

Listening and learning includes focused listening activities that help learners develop active listening skills, scan for details and draw inferences from what they have heard.

Speaking and practising has focused speaking activities that help learners develop fluency and accuracy in speaking, and hone their presentation skills.

Saying it right covers different aspects of phonics and pronunciation.

Word Wizard provides vocabulary support in the form of key words and phrases required for the task.

Grammar Guide provides language and grammar inputs to facilitate accurate language production.

Info byte provides quick tips and tricks about sounds and spoken language.

Manners matter! contains gestural and verbal clues that are vital for making the right impression while speaking.

Interacting and communicating includes integrated listening and speaking tasks; usually interactive pair and group work for students to practise and assess what they have learnt.

Fun Activity contains activities for enjoyment while learning.

Each book also has the following special features:

Dictation time provides additional practice for the learners' listening and spelling skills.

Take a break! are three well-designed activities that allow learners to refresh the topics learnt in the preceding chapters.

Saying it better! teaches common phrases and guides learners to avoid incorrect and colloquial language usage.

Children's Literary Fest is an art-integrated activity that focuses on increasing the learners' interest in literature.

How to use the book

Each chapter is based on a theme and focuses on a communicative function. Parents and teachers can initiate the learners into the theme of the chapter through the warm-up activity given in *Getting started*.

Chapter

Draw the student's attention to the learning objectives given at the beginning of the chapters. This would help them to focus on the key learning points of the chapter.

Do the listening and learning activities for developing active listening skills. Play the audio tracks at least twice for 'while-listening' and 'post-listening' tasks. During the first time, the students should be asked only to listen. When they listen to it for the second time, get them to complete the task. Give them clear instructions at the beginning of the tasks and check whether they understand what needs to be done.

Conduct the phonic drills and pronunciation activities with care. Get the students to listen and repeat the words and phrases multiple times till they get the pronunciation right. While this can be done as a class activity too, it would be best to monitor each student individually. Use the audio-visual input to learn the right way of making the English sounds.

When conducting the speaking activities, make sure all the students get a fair chance to participate. Demonstrate the task and check whether the students know how to do it. The presentation tips given for the activities in the *Manners matter!* boxes can be used to inculcate good habits and to build the right attitude required in students to make an impression when they speak.

For Assessment

Teachers can choose any of the listening and speaking activities for testing the students' achievement levels. It is, however, advisable to share the parameters of assessment with the students beforehand so that they know what is expected of them. Teachers can refer to the Teacher's Resource Books for this.

Teacher's Resource Books contain the lesson plans, teaching strategies and the answer keys besides the parameters of assessment for each task.

DigiSuite, the interactive digital resource pack, has the e-book with audio for the listening tasks, interactive activities and training videos demonstrating the right way of doing the speaking tasks.

We hope that teachers and students would find this series useful in developing listening and pronunciation and speaking skills and that it would enable students to become effective communicators in English.

Key to NEP tags and SDG icons

Revised Tune In! is a listening and speaking course that is closely aligned with the National Education Policy, 2020. It uses interactive approach, and experiential activities to build communicative competence in students. This series aims to prepare learners with the various skills outlined in the National Education Policy, 2020.

These skills have been tagged appropriately for the user's convenience. Here is the key to the tags.

India Focus NEP

- India Focus puts spotlight on the heritage, culture, customs, and history and geography of the Indian subcontinent.
- This provides students a deeper understanding of their homeland and creates a sense of solidarity.

Art Integration NEP

- Art Integrated Learning (AIL) is a teaching-learning model that integrates fine arts (painting, sculpture, architecture, music, and poetry), performing arts (theatre and dance), and photography with teaching new concepts.
- This provides students with an experiential and a multi-disciplinary learning experience.

Cross-curricular NEP

- The cross-curricular approach to a topic recognizes that all subjects are interlinked. It includes contributions from several different disciplines or viewpoints for effective learning.
- Certain activities cover cross-curricular content appropriate to that class.

Happiness Content NEP

- Learning should be an enjoyable process for learners. It should focus on building and understanding new concepts rather than rote learning.
- Children should experience happiness through learning and awareness, active participation in class, and also in their relationships with their friends and family.

Experiential Learning NEP

- Experiential learning is a process of learning through hands-on experience. Here, students 'learn by doing' an activity followed by reflective observation on the experience from multiple perspectives.
- This method helps learners link existing knowledge to understand new concepts and apply it to make decisions.

Twenty-First Century Skills

- The twenty-first century skills ensure that today's students can thrive in an ever-changing world and can use these skills to learn constantly.
- Here are the most commonly cited twenty-first century skills in this series:

Critical Thinking NEP

Communication Skills NEP

Collaboration NEP

Creativity NEP

Digital Literacy NEP

Sustainable Development Goals

- The Sustainable Development Goals, adopted by the United Nations in 2015, are a collection of 17 interlinked global goals designed to achieve a better and more sustainable future for all by 2030.
- Here are the 17 goals:

1 NO POVERTY
2 ZERO HUNGER
3 GOOD HEALTH AND WELL-BEING
4 QUALITY EDUCATION
5 GENDER EQUALITY
6 CLEAN WATER AND SANITATION
7 AFFORDABLE AND CLEAN ENERGY
8 DECENT WORK AND ECONOMIC GROWTH
9 INDUSTRY, INNOVATION AND INFRASTRUCTURE
10 REDUCED INEQUALITIES
11 SUSTAINABLE CITIES AND COMMUNITIES
12 RESPONSIBLE CONSUMPTION AND PRODUCTION
13 CLIMATE ACTION
14 LIFE BELOW WATER
15 LIFE ON LAND
16 PEACE, JUSTICE AND STRONG INSTITUTIONS
17 PARTNERSHIPS FOR THE GOALS

Detailed Contents

Chapter	Listening and learning	Speaking and practising	Saying it right & Dictation time	Interacting and communicating	Fun *Activity*
1. Describing daily routine (*Communicative functions:* identifying food with time; learning to locate specific information; understanding the information in a text accurately; talking about one's daily routine)	Listening to conversations about everyday actions and routines, and filling gaps, and identifying statements as true or false	*Pair work:* asking and answering questions about daily routine; talking about one's daily routine; *pair work*: describing one's routine on a holiday	Listening to a song and singing along; listening to a conversation and writing the speakers' favourite things; listening and identifying words with *p* and *b* sounds Listening and gap-filling	Asking one's teacher about their daily routine; *Group work:* discussing one's grandparents' daily routine.	*Asking a fruit* vendor or an ice cream seller about their daily routine, discussing it in class
2. Introducing people (*Communicative functions:* asking questions to gather information; introducing one's friends; listening and locating specific information; describing people)	Listening to conversations to write the speakers' names, and to match people to their skills	Listening to a person's description; describing a friend or a family member; describing people shown in pictures	Listening to a song and singing along; practising words with *t* and *d* sounds and sorting them Listening and gap-filling	Completing a conversation with specific information; *pair work:* introducing a family member or relative to a friend	Describing a famous person, and guessing your classmates' description
3. Helping at home (*Communicative functions:* talking about housework; asking for and offering help)	Listening to people asking for and offering help and filling a table; listening to a conversation and identifying correct options	*Role-play:* listening to conversations and enacting them; asking for help in different situations; offering help to people in situations shown in pictures	Listening to a song and singing along; practising and sorting words with the *k* sound and different *g* sounds Listening and gap-filling	*Pair work:* asking for and offering help in different situations	Narrating a story to your class about people helping each other
Take a break!					
4. Around the neighbourhood (*Communicative functions:* talking about locations; giving directions and responding to directions)	Listening to the description of a neighbourhood and identifying places there; listening to a person giving directions and gap-filling	*Pair work:* reading a conversation and asking and answering questions about places in a market	*Group work:* playing the game Name, Place, Animal, Thing; practising words with *m* and *n* sounds Listening and gap-filling	*Role play:* listening to directions to a place, following the route on a map and giving directions to a place in one's neighbourhood; *pair work:* talking about the locations of places in a neighbourhood	*Pair work:* giving directions to reach the destination through a maze and tracing the path
5. Let's be safe. (*Communicative functions:* identifying and talking about safe and unsafe objects in and around the house, and safety on the road; expressing one's feelings of pain and fear)	Listening to conversations and sorting safe and unsafe things, and marking safe and unsafe places in a picture	*Group work:* reading a conversation on road safety and discussing more ways of ensuring safety on the road; *pair work:* discussing the meanings of various road signs	Listening to a song and singing along; practising words with *v* and *w* sounds Listening and gap-filling	*Pair work:* listening to a conversation, filling gaps and having a similar conversation; writing words expressing pain and fear	*Survey:* Asking ten classmates about things that they are scared of
6. At the bus stop (*Communicative functions:* requesting information; offering and accepting help; accepting/refusing things politely)	Listening to conversations at a bus stop and answering questions, and filling in a table	*Role-play:* reading and enacting a conversation on offering, accepting and refusing help politely	Listening to a song and singing along; practising and sorting words ending in *s* or *es* Listening and gap-filling	*Group work:* discussing how one can ask for information at a railway station	Filling in a Help Diary
Take a break!					

Chapter	Listening and learning	Speaking and practising	Saying it right & Dictation time	Interacting and communicating	Fun Activity
7. **I can do it.** (*Communicative functions:* describing different skills that people have; reporting a conversation using your own words)	Listening to conversations and filling in a table; discussing the subject of the conversation and completing a report	*Group work:* reading a conversation and having a similar conversation; telling one's classmates about a memorable evening	Listening to a song and singing along; listening for and practising words with the *ng* sound Listening and gap-filling	*Pair work:* listening to a conversation and discussing the plan for an event at school; *group work:* asking classmates about what they want to do for Teacher's Day and writing their responses; planning a party, saying what one can and cannot do	*Group work:* talking about the different ways you could take care of stray animals
8. **How's the day today?** (*Communicative functions:* describing the weather; talking about holidays/leisure activities)	Listening to conversations and sorting statements, and answering questions	*Group work:* reading a conversation and asking and answering questions about favourite days and activities; speaking about one's favourite leisure activity	Listening to a song and singing along; listening to and practising words ending in *f* and their plurals Listening and gap-filling	Conducting a survey on your classmates' favourite weather	Completing names of some famous in India
9. **It's playtime!** (*Communicative functions:* talking about simple everyday; talking about the rules of various sports; learning to match oral descriptions with images)	Listening to the rules of a game and completing sentences using *can* and *cannot*; listening to a conversation and matching people's names with the pictures showing their favourite leisure activities	*Pair work:* reading a conversation and reporting it in one's own words; asking and answering questions about the rules of hopscotch; talking about different games	Listening to a song and singing along; practising words with the *ch* sound; practising words with the consonant sound *y* Listening and gap-filling	*Group work:* describing the rules of *Ludo* to the class and playing the game	*Group work:* Playing a game of *Chinese Whispers*
Take a break!					
10. **What's happening?** (*Communicative functions:* describing and talking about current actions and events, asking and answering questions, and framing meaningful sentences using the continuous tense)	Listening to a description of people's actions and matching the pictures of people with their actions; listening to a recipe and writing down the ingredients used, and ticking the correct options	*Pair work:* describing the activities of one's classmates; asking and answering questions about the activities of people and animals listed; describing people's activities in a park	Listening to a song and singing along; practising words with the two different sounds of *th* Listening and gap-filling	*Group work:* asking and answering questions about the activities shown in a picture	Playing a game using a dice
11. **How will it be?** (*Communicative functions:* learning words to plan a holiday; taking quick decisions and talking about planned events in the future tense)	Listening to conversations and identifying statements as true or false and answering questions	*Pair work:* talking about actions that will take place in the future; *role-play:* reenacting a conversation; reading a conversation and matching statements with suitable responses	Listening to a song and singing along; practising words with short and long vowel sounds and sorting them correctly Listening and gap-filling	*Pair work:* describing a travel itinerary using the future tense	Sharing one's itinerary for the summer vacation with the class
Saying it better!					
Children's Literary Fest					

Contents

1 Describing daily routine

In this chapter, we will:

- learn to identify food with time.
- listen and learn to locate specific information.
- learn to understand the information in a text accurately.
- learn to talk about our daily routine.
- learn to differentiate between the p and b sounds.

Getting started

Cross-curricular NEP

A. *Identify* **These pictures show different foods. Write (b) for breakfast, (l) for lunch and (d) for dinner to show when you have it.**

....

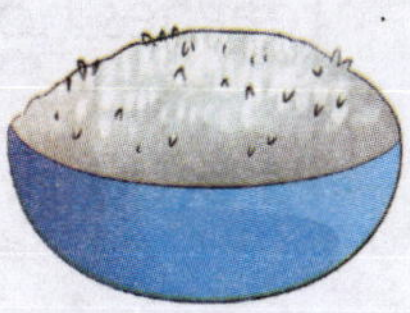

....

....

Listening and learning

B1. *Listen*

Listen to Snehal talking to her new neighbour, Mrs Sinha, in the park.

B2. *Gap-fill*

Listen again. Fill in the missing information.

1. .... is Snehal's new neighbour.
2. .... is the time when Snehal reaches home from school.
3. At 5:00 p.m. Snehal ....
4. Snehal .... before she comes down to play.
5. Mrs Sinha bakes ....
6. .... is the place where Mrs Sinha invites Snehal.

B3. *True or false* 1.3

Snehal wants to know how Mrs Sinha spends her time. Listen to what she finds out.

Now, read the following sentences about the daily routine of Mrs Sinha. Write (T) for true and (F) for false.

1. Mrs Sinha does not go to office. ☐
2. She has a lot of free time. ☐
3. She does yoga in the evening. ☐
4. Her kids go to school at 7:00 a.m. ☐
5. She has lunch at 1:30 p.m. ☐
6. She bakes cookies and cakes after lunch. ☐
7. She sells cookies and cakes to supermarkets. ☐
8. She helps her kids with their homework. ☐
9. She goes to bed at 11:00 p.m. ☐

Speaking and practising

3 GOOD HEALTH AND WELL-BEING

C1. *Ask and answer*

1.4

The things that you do around the same time every day is called your 'daily routine'. Now, listen to Ashwin talk about his daily routine.

Manners matter!

After we ask a question, we should pay attention to what the other person is replying to us. We should try to make them feel comfortable answering our questions.

Collaboration NEP

Work in pairs. Take turns to ask your partner these questions and write their response.

1. When do you wake up in the morning?

   ....

2. When do you eat breakfast?

   ....

3. When do you eat lunch?

   ....

4. What do you do in the evening?

   ....

5. When do you study?

   ....

6. When do you go to bed?

   ....

Collaboration NEP

C2. *Talk*

Read the following speech where a teacher talks about her daily routine.

Now, with the help of the speech above, talk about your daily routine with your partner.

Collaboration NEP

C3. *Share*

How do you spend your holiday? Is it just like your school day?

Tell your partner what you do on a holiday.

Saying it right

Art Integration NEP

D1. *Sing*

Listen to the song and sing along.

My pet bat's name is Pat;
Pat, the bat is his name!

He picks at plums and eats big bugs;
Pat, the bat is his name!

D2. *Listen*

Here are two friends, Penny and Benny. Listen to them talking about their favourite things.

D3. *List*

In pairs, list the different things that Penny and Benny like.

Penny likes...	Benny likes...

D4. *Identify*

Read the following sentences aloud. Underline the words with p sound and circle the words with b sound.

1. There's a big, blue bug on the purple plate.
2. The boy dropped the burnt bun.
3. Billy pulled all the black buttons off his shirt.
4. The brown bear pulled a pin out of its paw.
5. The pink panther played with pots and pans.

Dictation time

E. *Listen and write*

Listen and fill in the blanks.

We must have ....
to keep our body fit. It will also keep us
.... As children, we love
.... We
may eat them but ....!

3 GOOD HEALTH AND WELL-BEING

Interacting and communicating

F1. *Ask*

Ask your teacher about his/her daily routine.

F2. *Discuss*

Ask your grandparents how they spend their day. Do they go to work like your father/ mother or spend their time at home?

Fun Activity

Ask a fruit vendor or an ice cream seller about his daily routine. Is his daily routine different from yours? Discuss in class.

2 Introducing people

In this chapter, we will:

- learn to ask questions and gather information.
- learn to introduce friends.
- learn to listen and locate specific information.
- learn to describe people.
- learn to differentiate between the t and d sounds.

Getting started

A. *Ask and answer* **Work in pairs. Ask your partner the following questions and note down his/her answers.**

1. What is your name?	6. Who is your favourite actor?
2. When is your birthday?	7. Which is your favourite book?
3. Which is your favourite colour?	8. What is your favourite season?
4. Which is your favourite game/sport?	9. Who is your idol/role model?
5. Which is your favourite food?	10. Where do you live?

Listening and learning

B1. *Listen* 2.1 **Abdul has joined a new school and is meeting his classmates for the first time. Listen to their conversation.**

B2. *Identify* 2.2

Now, listen to the conversation again and write the names of the students in the table below. Use the clues given in the pictures.

Old Student	New Student	Old Student	Old Student
III B	III B	III B	III A
Name:	Name:	Name:	Name: ....

B3. *Listen* 2.3

Smitha is showing Benji her album. Listen to their conversation.

B4. *Listen* 2.4

Listen to the conversation again and match the people to their skills.

Sanjay Siraj Sunitha Rima

learns karate | learns Carnatic music | learns Kathak | plays cricket

Speaking and practising

C1. *Describe* 2.5

Listen to how Tanya is describing her cousin Soumil.

Manners matter!

When we describe someone, we give the following details:

Age
Height
Body build
Shape of face
Colour of hair/eyes
Activties they enjoy

Now, describe a friend or a family member.

Grammar Guide: Interesting language points

You may use the following sentence structure to describe someone:

This is my .... She/He is years old. She/He has .... face. Her/His eyes are .... She/He likes to .... and ....

C2. *Describe*

Describe these people.

Mrs Jha

Ms Rachel

Master Vishal

Word Wizard: Useful words and phrases

You may use these words in your description:

sixty/ten/forty years

dark/deep/pale/blue/ brown eyes

long/curly/straight hair

bun/plait/pony tail

dark/fair/wheatish complexion

loves painting/playing cricket/playing guitar

slim/plump/medium build

Saying it right

Art Integration NEP

D1. *Sing* **Listen to the song and sing along.**

2.6

Ten tin tops

Twelve teddy bears

Come, let us play,

And all the toys we'll share!

D2. *Say aloud* **Label the pictures. Then, say the words aloud.**

....

....

D3. *Mark*

Listen to the words. Put a star (☆) for the words with t sound and a smiley (☺) for the words with d sound. Count the stars and smileys. How many of each did you get?

tin	din	two
dull	team	dim
damp	dump	team
dumb	tennis	tomato

Dictation time

E. *Listen and write*

Listen and fill in the blanks.

4 QUALITY EDUCATION

We must .... But we must .... too.

.... make our body fit and our mind sharp. Remember,

....

makes Jack a dull boy.

Interacting and communicating

Communication Skills NEP

F1. *Complete*

You are Tenzin Sonam. Nadeem, a new student, has joined your class recently. You want to introduce Nadeem to three of your friends. Complete the conversation.

Sonam: Hi friends, this is Nadeem. He has just joined our school.

Munpreet: Hi Nadeem, I am Munpreet. So you are in III A. I'm in ....

Nadeem: Hi Munpreet. Yes, and I sit with ....

Sonam: Nadeem, this is Soha. She's from .... She loves to play basketball.

Nadeem: Hi Soha, I love playing .... too.

Sonam:	And Nadeem, this is .... He's from .... He goes home by the school bus.
Nadeem:	Hi Sunil, I go home by the school bus too. I take bus no. 15. What about you?
Sunil:	Mine is bus no. ....
Nadeem:	I am so happy to meet all of you. I'll not feel lonely at all now!
Everyone:	We are .... to meet you too. Bye, then. See you around.

F2. *Introduce* **Introduce a family member or relative to a friend.**

Fun Activity

Collaboration • Communication Skills NEP

Form two teams. Choose a well-known actor/sportsperson. Describe him or her without saying the name. The other team has to guess who the person is. The team which makes the most number of correct guesses is the winner.

3 Helping at home

In this chapter, we will:

- learn to listen and identify specific information.
- learn to ask for and offer help.
- learn to differentiate between k and g sounds.

Getting started

A. *Identify* **Here is a list of household chores. Who does these chores at your home? Write the person's name against each chore. At the end, write one chore that you do at home.**

1. Going to the grocer's
   ....
2. Waters the flowerpots
   ....
3. Folds clothes
   ....
4. Helps in the kitchen
   ....
5. Packs your lunch
   ....
6. Drops you to school or at the bust stop
   ....
7. Buys vegetables/fruits
   ....

I do .... at home.

Listening and learning

B1. *Listen* 3.1

Imagine that your teacher needs help with a few things in class. Some of you are helping her. Listen to the conversation.

B2. *Gap-fill* 3.2

Now, listen to the conversation again. Fill in the missing information in the table below. You can listen to the conversation one more time, if required.

Help needed	Person offering help
....	Ashyr
collecting diaries	....
....	Atharv
minding the class	....

B3. *Choose* 3.3

Your mother will be away from home for two days. Listen to how she has arranged for the chores to be divided among your grandparents, father, sister and you.

Now, read the sentences below and underline the correct options.

1. *Father/Grandfather* will get the vegetables.
2. *Mother/Grandmother* will make breakfast.
3. You and your sister will *take the dog for a walk/water the flowerpots.*

4. Your *teacher/Grandfather* will help you with your homework.
5. Grandmother and Father will make *dinner/a cake* together.
6. After dinner, you will *watch TV/go for a walk*.
7. *Grandmother/Father* will help you get ready for school.
8. Mother thinks that they will *miss her very much/have a lot of fun*.

Speaking and practising

Collaboration NEP

C1. *Role-play* 3.4

Listen to the two conversations between a salesgirl and a shopper; and Amit and his grandmother. Then, role-play the conversations with your partner.

Manners matter!

Three Magic Words!

When you ask for something, always say, 'please!'
When someone does something for you, never forget to say, 'Thank you!'
When someone thanks you for doing something, always say, 'You're welcome!'

Grammar Guide: Interesting language points

When we ask for or offer help, we say:

May I ...., please?

Can I/you ...., please?

Could I/you ...., please?

Examples:

Could you help me lift the box, please?

May I help you open the door?

When we respond to someone's request for help, we say:

Sure, I will. *Yes, I can.* *Certainly.*

C2. *Ask*

Read the following situations. How would you ask for help?

1. You have left your house keys behind in your school, inside your desk's drawer. You need to call your mother. How will you ask your neighbour for help?
2. You were absent from school for two days. You need to complete your work. How will you ask your friend for his notes?
3. Your friend's father has bought her a new computer game. You want her to let you play it on her computer. How will you ask her for it?

C3. *Offer*

Look at these pictures where different people need help. How will you offer them help?

a.

b.

c.

d.

e.

C4. *Role-play* **Aatif and Dhani's parents will not be home on Saturday. Read the list of household chores they have given Aatif and Dhani.**

5 GENDER EQUALITY

Aatif	Dhani
1. Wash the dishes	1. Arrange the newspapers
2. Put the toys away tidily	2. Put the dirty laundry in the washing machine
3. Arrange books on the bookshelf	3. Stack the folded clothes in the almirah
4. Polish his school shoes	4. Water the plants kept indoors
5. Fold the dry clothes	5. Stack the washed dishes in the cupboard

Work in pairs. Imagine you and your partner are Aatif and Dhani. Ask for and offer each other help with the chores that are assigned to you.

Saying it right

D1. *Sing*

3.5

Listen to the song and sing along.

Kites and gems.
Kites and gems.
I fly kites,
I buy gems.
Kites are beautiful,
Gems are precious,
Pretty real kites!
Lovely costly gems!

D2. *Repeat*

3.6

Listen to the pronunciation of these words and repeat them.

kid	kick	kilo	kind	kiss
king	kit	kitchen	kettle	kart
girl	gift	goat	golf	guitar
gel	gem	giant	giraffe	ginger

Did you notice the sound made by k in the first two rows?

What sound does g make in the last two rows? Is there a difference in its sound?

D3. *Sort* 3.7

Listen to the words again. Then, write the words in the correct columns.

k **as in *key***	***g*** **as in *gun***	***g*** **as in *gem***

Dictation time

E. *Listen and write* DT

Listen and fill in the blanks.

5 GENDER EQUALITY

.... at home is a good habit. At my home, my father helps .... while my mother helps .... around the house. My brother and I .... and ....

Interacting and communicating

Critical Thinking NEP

F. *Discuss*

Read the following situations. Then, take turns and discuss with your partner how you would complete the following tasks.

1. It's sports day at school. You and your friend are arranging the prizes and gifts. How will you help each other?
2. It's your brother's birthday. You and your father are decorating the house. How will you help each other?

Word Wizard: Useful words and phrases

You may use the following words to talk about the tasks:

scissors	decorations	gift wrap
gum	tape	table
books	pens	medals
balloons	cakes	cold drinks
stack	knife	cut
hang	paste	snacks

Fun Activity

Do you know any stories about people helping each other? Narrate a story in the class.

TAKE a break

Mindful Cooking

Experiential Learning • Happiness Content NEP

Cooking is a skill that we must learn. Try to make a simple dish at home, such as a sandwich. Ask for help when using cutlery and appliances. Think of these questions when you make it:

- What are you making?
- How do the ingredients taste?
- How do the ingredients feel in your hand?
- Do the ingredients have their distinct aroma?
- Are there any sounds—ping of the microwave or sizzle of the pan?

Describe this experience to your classmate. Include the answers to the questions given above in your description. Listen to your classmate's experience as well.

4 Around the neighbourhood

In this chapter, we will:

- learn to listen for details.
- learn to ask for, give and follow directions.
- learn to differentiate between the m and n sounds.

Getting started

Art Integration NEP

A. *Sing* 4.1

Listen to the song and sing along.

I love my neighbourhood,
It has everything I need.
There's a park,
Where sings a lark.
It has a school,
Which has a pool.
There's a bakery,
There's a nursery.
I love my neighbourhood,
It has everything I need!

Listening and learning

B1. *Listen* 4.2

Chandu has recently shifted to Green Valley Apartments. He talks to Niyati and finds out about his new neighbourhood. Listen to their conversation.

B2. *Identify* 4.3

Listen to the conversation again. Put a tick (✓) against the places that are found in the neighbourhood.

11 SUSTAINABLE CITIES AND COMMUNITIES

vegetable market	☐	library	☐
toy store	☐	bakery	☐
shopping mall	☐	railway station	☐
bus stop	☐	police station	☐
supermarket	☐	bookshop	☐
school	☐	hospital	☐
post-office	☐	clothes store	☐

B3. *Gap-fill*

4.4

Chandu wants to go to the bakery to buy some bread. Listen to Niyati giving him directions and fill in the blanks.

Go straight. Take the .... right turn. Walk .... steps ahead. Then, enter the .... lane to your .... The fourth shop painted in .... is the bakery.

Speaking and practising

C1. *Read*

Read this conversation.

Chandu: Hi Niyati! I want to buy a pencil and a sharpener. Where can I get them?

Niyati: Oh, you can go to the bookshop nearby.

Chandu: Where is it?

Niyati: It's right across the road, the big, green shop beside the medical shop.

Chandu: Thank you, Niyati.

Communication Skills NEP

C2. *Ask and answer*

Now work in pairs. Ask and answer questions about the location of these shops and the things you get there.

supermarket	toy store	shoe shop
bakery	medical shop	

Word Wizard: Useful words and phrases

You can use the following sentences to answer the questions:

It's the green building on the ground floor.

It's the second shop on the left.

It's quite close by.

It's the biggest shop on that road.

It's quite far.

Saying it right

D1. *Play*

Have you ever played a game of Name, Place, Animal, Thing?

In this game, players come up with a name, a place, an animal or a bird, and a thing that starts with a specific letter of the alphabet, in 30 seconds.

Info byte

The letters **m** and **n** make the sounds '**mmm**' and '**nnn**' which are nasal sounds. Nasal sounds can only be made when air passes through your nose.

Try saying '**mmm**' and '**nnn**' a couple of times. Now pinch your nose, and try saying the two sounds. Can you still make the sounds?

Play two rounds of Name, Place, Animal, Thing for the letters m and n. Your teacher will help you keep track of the time.

After you have finished the two rounds, take turns reading aloud the different words that you have written.

Letter	Name	Place	Animal	Thing
a	Asin	Amritsar	ape	apple
m				
n				

D2. *Repeat*

4.5

Listen to the following sentences carefully. Pay attention to where the m and n sounds are in each word when you repeat the sentences.

1. The monkeys made much mess.
2. I love eating yummy tomato jam.
3. Tim likes gum, jam and ham.
4. Nice nurses are never noisy.
5. Honey, the bunny, was running down the road.
6. This man has a clean, green lawn.

D3. *Complete*

Work in groups of five. Read aloud the sentences given below and complete them with suitable words from the box.

clean	Sam	tomato	nest
muffins	hammer	Tom	lamb
camel	nurse	win	milk
run	more	nail	coin

1. Make me some ....
   ....
   (a word that begins with *m*)
2. Mary has a ....
   ....
   (words with *m* in the middle)
3. Come home, ...
   ....
   (names of people that end with *m*)
4. Never nudge a ....
   ....
   (words that begin with *n*)
5. Anitha likes to ....
   (an action word that end with *n*)

Dictation time

E. *Listen and write* DT

Listen and fill in the blanks.

11 SUSTAINABLE CITIES AND COMMUNITIES

We live in a .... that has everything—a ...., a ...., a .... and a .... We have big .... for all the children to play in. We keep our surroundings ....

Interacting and communicating

Communication Skills · Art Integration NEP

F1. *Role-play* 4.6

This is a picture map of Neha's neighbourhood. Nitin is new to the neighbourhood. Listen to Neha giving Nitin directions to the post office. Then, role-play a similar conversation with your partner, giving him/her directions to a place in your neighbourhood.

F2. *Follow*

Where does Nitin want to go? Listen to the conversation again and trace the route that Neha tells Nitin to take on the map of the neighbourhood.

Art Integration NEP

F3. *Talk*

In pairs, take turns imagining you are Nitin and Neha, and talk about the location of the following places.

- library
- police station
- school
- Neha's house
- fire station

Example:

Nitin: Where is the library?

Neha: The library is opposite to the colony park, which is next to your house.

Fun Activity

Critical Thinking • Collaboration NEP

Work in pairs and help the bear find its den. Tell your partner the way to the den. Your partner will draw it.

5 Let's be safe.

In this chapter, we will:

- learn to listen for and identify necessary information.
- learn to speak about road safety.
- learn to differentiate between the v and w sounds.
- learn to talk about things that scare us.

Getting started

Critical Thinking NEP

A. *Identify* **Look at the objects on the table. Circle the ones that eight-year-old Meena should play with.**

Listening and learning

B1. *Listen* 5.1

Tarun wants to play inside the house. Listen to the conversation between Tarun and his mother.

B2. *Complete* 5.2

Listen to the conversation again and complete the following table.

Safe	Not safe

B3. *Listen* 5.3

Bonny and Kiran want to play in Mr Sharma's garden. Listen to Mr Sharma telling them where they can play.

B4. *Mark* 5.4

Now look at the picture of Mr Sharma's garden. In which places are Bonny and Kiran allowed to play? Listen and tick (✓) the correct boxes.

Speaking and practising

Communication Skills NEP

C1. *Role-play* **Ten-year-old Jasmine is going to visit her grandparents with her brother Robin, who is fifteen. Their mother is talking to them about how to be safe on the road. Read the conversation.**

Mother:	Listen, Jasmine and Robin. Be careful on the road. Do not get off a running bus. Wait till the bus stops completely.
Robin and Jasmine:	Okay, Mummy.
Mother:	And be careful while crossing the road. Cross it only at the zebra crossing.
Robin and Jasmine:	Okay, Mummy. We'll be careful.
Mother:	I'm scared that you'll get hurt if you aren't careful. And, Robin, take care of your sister. Do not let her ....

What else would you tell Robin and Jasmine about road safety? Form groups of three. Think of some more road safety rules. Then, act out the roles of the mother, Robin and Jasmine. You can look at the pictures in the next page for more ideas.

Top Ten Road Safety Tips for Children

1. Crossing the road.

Look both ways and listen for traffic before crossing. Always use the zebra crossing. Never run on the road.

2. Knowing the signals for people.

There are traffic signals for people as well. We must walk when it shows the walk signal. We must not *walk* when it shows the *stop* signal.

3. Knowing the signals.

Green means vehicles can move.

Red means they have to stop.

Yellow means they have to slow down.

4. Watching out for big cars.

Stay away from vehicles turning the corner.

5. Never sticking your hands outside a vehicle.

You can be hit by vehicles speeding past or going in the opposite direction.

6. Getting off a vehicle.

Never get off a moving vehicle. Watch out for cars or motorcycles when getting off.

7. Always using pavements.

Do not walk on the road, use the pavement.

8. Wear a seatbelt.

Always wear the seatbelt while seated in a vehicle.

9. Not playing between cars stationed side by side.

Do not play behind cars that are parked.

10. Using safety gear on bicycles and skates.

Never ride bicycles or skates without wearing your safety gear. Use bicycle lanes when available.

C2. *Discuss* **Work in pairs. Here are some road signs. Do you know what they mean? Discuss with your partner.**

Elderly people

School crossing

Pedestrian crossing

Level crossing without barrier

Level crossing with barrier

Low-flying aircraft

Cycle route ahead

Trams crossing

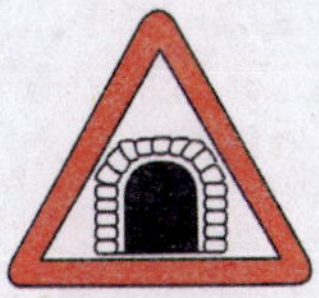
Tunnel ahead

Pedestrians in road

Risk of grounding

Queues likely

Saying it right

Art Integration NEP

D1. *Sing* **Listen to the song and sing along.**

5.5

Oh my puppy,
My poor pet,
You're hurt,
You're wet.
And, you have a wound!
Wait, I'll wrap it around.
I'll take you to the vet, quickly in my van,
Don't you worry, and don't you run!
You'll soon be well, to play in the sun.
Pain will go.
Don't you cry, not anymore!
You'll soon be well, it won't be sore.

D2. *Repeat*

5.6

Listen to these words and repeat them.

Set A

wall	warm	wash	watch
water	whale	wet	wheel
wheat	what	window	wind

Now, listen to these words and repeat them.

Set B

van	vase	vegetable	very
vest	vet	video	village
violet	violin	vast	voice

Did you notice any difference in the way the two sets of words are pronounced?

Here is the difference.

Set A	Set B
When you say *wet* or *water*, you circle your lips and your lips become round.	When you say *vet* or *van*, you touch your lower lip with your upper teeth.

D3. *Read aloud*

Now listen to both kinds of words. Practise saying them aloud.

5.7

walk	waist	want	way
well	west	wheat	when
whisper	white	wing	which
vehicle	value	vacation	vanilla
vanish	vapour	variety	visit

D4. *Say aloud*

Say aloud the following words. Is the w being pronounced?

5.8

wrap	wreath	wrench	wrestler
wriggle	wring	write	wrong

Which sound do you hear in place of the w sound?

Work with a partner and find six more words where w is not pronounced.

Dictation time

E. *Listen and write*

DT

Listen and fill in the blanks.

13 CLIMATE ACTION

Everyone loves to light .... in Diwali. But have you thought about ....? We must not .... them. They cause .... Bursting firecrackers also .... It often harms ....

Interacting and communicating

Communication Skills • Collaboration NEP

F1. *Talk* 5.9

Megha and Manoj are siblings. Listen to them talk about a scary film they watched on the TV. Then, work in pairs and talk to your partner about a film that you have watched recently.

F2. *Complete* 5.10

Listen to the conversation and complete these sentences.

1. Megha is scared of ....
2. Manoj is afraid of ....
3. The little boy in the film ....

Experiential Learning NEP

F3. *Share*

Are you scared of something? What is it? Tell your friend. Find out from him/her what he/she is afraid of.

F4. *Find words* **Here are some words related to pain and fear. Think of another word related to these emotions. Then, express that word on a blank sheet of paper.**

frightened	hurt	terrified

Fun Activity

Go around the class. Find out from at least ten of your classmates what they are scared of.

6 At the bus stop

In this chapter, we will:

- learn to ask for information.
- learn to offer, accept or refuse help.
- learn to pronounce the ending sound of plurals with s or es.

Getting started

Critical Thinking NEP

A. *Match* **Whom will you ask these questions at a bus stop? Match the questions with the people.**

1. What time will the bus arrive?	a. Driver
2. Can I go to the washroom?	b. Conductor
3. What is the price of a ticket?	c. Inquiry officer
4. Which is the next stop?	d. Your parent

Listening and learning

B1. *Listen* 6.1 **Suraj and his father, Mr Sinha, are going to Suraj's grandparents' house. Their bus is at 6:00 p.m. It's now 5:50 p.m. Listen to what is happening.**

B2. *Answer*

Listen to the conversation again. Answer the following questions.

1. What time do Suraj and Mr Sinha reach the bus stop?

   ....

2. Where are they going? Why?

   ....

3. Are they late? How can you say so?

   ....

4. What is the correct time of departure?

   ....

5. Has the bus left already? How do they find out whether the bus had left?

   ....

6. At which stop will the bus arrive today?

   ....

7. Does Mr Sinha allow Suraj to carry the bag? Why/Why not?

   ....

8. Is the inquiry officer a polite man? How do you know?

   ....

B3. *Listen*

Suraj and Mr Sinha are now going towards stop no. 78. Listen to what is happening.

B4. *Complete*

Listen to the conversation again. Then, fill in the information about who offers to help and if the offer is accepted.

Offer of help	Offered by	Accepted/ refused
Call a porter	Suraj	Accepted

Speaking and practising

Collaboration NEP

C1. *Role-play*

Read the following conversation. Then, enact a similar conversation with your partner, offering and accepting help. If you do not need help, then refuse the offer politely.

Manners matter!

Refusing offer of help

When someone has offered you help and you do not need it, refuse it politely. You can say, 'Thank you very much for your offer but I can do it on my own.'

Collaboration NEP

C2. *Offer help*

Look at these pictures. Then, in pairs, role-play the situations. Asking for, offering and accepting help.

Example:

Student 1: Can I help you carry the books?

Student 2: Yes, please, that would be very helpful.

a. 

b. 

e. 

c. 

d. 

Word Wizard: Useful words and phrases

Here are some phrases which you can use when offering help to someone:

- I'll... (do something)
  Example: I'll carry the bag for you.
- Let me... (do something)
  Example: Let me open the door for you.
- Do you want me to... (do something)
  Example: Do you want me to bring a glass of water for you?
- Would you like me to... (do something)
  Example: Would you like me to carry the books?

Saying it right

Art Integration NEP

D1. *Sing* 6.5

Listen to this song and sing along.

Cats and rats
Beds and bugs
Bridges and ledges
Are they friends?
Are they enemies?
Teachers and mummies
Tell me please!

D2. *Repeat*

6.6

Listen to the words. Repeat them. Notice how we pronounce the ending sound of a plural with s or es. There are three different ways of saying it.

[s] sound

cats	maps	racks	puffs

[z] sound

dogs	beds	bags	bells

[iz] sound

watches	bridges	judges	slices

D3. *Sort*

6.7

Listen to these words. Put them in the correct columns based on the sound of s you hear.

rats	tops	packs	matches
punches	slices	cubs	clouds
mugs	heels	bugs	dolls
boxes	maps	pixies	elves

s **as in** ***cats [s]***	***s*** **as in** ***dogs [z]***	***es*** **as in** ***bridges [iz]***

Dictation time

E. *Listen and write* DT

Listen and fill in the blanks.

Tanya's grandparents live ....

...., Tanya goes to visit them. She takes .... Her grandmother makes .... for her. Tanya thanks her .... and eats all the *pitta* ....

Interacting and communicating

Collaboration • Creativity NEP

F. *Discuss*

Work in small groups. Imagine you are at a railway station. Discuss how you will ask for information there. Then, share your ideas with the whole class.

Fun Activity

Experiential Learning NEP

Think of all the moments when you offered help to different people during the week. Fill in the details in the Help Diary below.

Help offered	To	Day
1. Folding clothes	Mummy	Monday

TAKE a break

Travel Time

Have you travelled anywhere recently? How did you travel there—by bus, train or airplane? Team up with your classmate and take turns to share your travel experience. Think of these questions when you describe your account.

- If you booked an airplane, where did you get to sit—at the window seat, in the middle or at the aisle seat?
- If you took the train, which berth did you get—upper, middle or lower? Did you travel in a coupé?
- How were the seats/berths—comfortable or uncomfortable? Why?
- Did the bus/train/airplane stop anywhere in between?
- What did you see inside the bus/train/airplane?
- How was the view outside?
- Would you like to travel in that mode of transportation again? Why/why not?

Listen to your partner's account and sketch a scene from his/her journey. Then, show it to your partner and ask him if the picture is as per the description.

7 I can do it.

In this chapter, we will:

- learn to talk about the different skills that people have.
- learn to report a conversation using our own words.
- learn to identify words with the ng sound.

Getting started

Cross-curricular NEP

A. *Write* | **Look at these pictures. Write the names of the activities and the people you know who can do these things.**

Painting: Ajit ....

....

....

....

....

....

Listening and learning

B1. *Listen*

Rohan is studying in Class 3. As a part of his group project, he has to ask three friends about things they are good at and things in which they need to improve. Listen to their conversation.

B2. *Complete*

Listen to the conversation between Rohan and his friends again. Then, complete the table below.

Person	**Can do**	**Can't do**	**Any other information**
Rohan			
Divya			
Mir			
Lata			

B3. *Listen* 7.3

Mir, Lata, Divya and Rohan regularly meet at the playground. Rohan and Lata are in Class 3. Mir is in Class 4, while Divya is in Class 5. They are studying in different schools. Listen to their conversation. What are they talking about?

B4. *Complete* 7.4

Mir goes back home and tells his mother about the evening with his friends. Listen to the conversation again and complete Mir's report.

Mummy, you know that my .... exams are in two weeks, right? But .... still writing the unit test 2 exams. All of us went to the playground at the usual time except .... Rohan told us that she had to .... You know that they both stay in the same .... But she joined us later. It seems her .... had a fall in the bathroom. She needs to take rest for .... We all decided to be careful when we .... too! By the way mummy, there is an .... in our locality. We are all planning to go there this .... Is it okay for us to go on our own? I promise we'll be careful.

Speaking and practising

Communication Skills NEP

C1. *Ask* **Read this conversation between Gaurav and his grandfather.**

Grandpa: Gaurav, can you get me my walking stick, please?

Gaurav: Yes, Grandpa. Here it is. Please take it.

Grandpa: How are you preparing for your exams? Your exams are round the corner, aren't they?

Gaurav: Yes, Grandpa. I'm confident of Maths. I can do the sums well and fast too. But I'm worried about EVS. I cannot draw the diagrams. I find them tough.

Now, form groups of three. Ask questions to find out which subject each one of you are confident about doing well in the exams.

C2. *Talk* **Remember how Mir told his mother about his evening with his friends. Tell your class about one such evening with your friends.**

Saying it right

Art Integration NEP

D1. *Sing* **Listen to this song and sing along.**

7.5

Once there was a strong, young king.
In his kingdom, it was always spring!
'Sing a song for me,' said he.
Cling clang went the drum!
Ding dong went the gong!
Still, 'Sing a song for me,' said he!
The king then got a bird to sing.
He gave it a shiny golden ring.
'Bring the bird,' said the king,
'Sing a song,' said the king.
The bird sang, 'Ting a ling!'

Info byte

Did you notice the **ng** sounds in the song? It is a nasal sound, like '**m**' and '**n**'. While '**n**' and '**g**' sounds are different, they come together to form the **ng** sound.

Read the song again on your own. What were the different ng sound words in the song? Write them in the box and read them aloud.

D2. *Form new words*

The ng sound joins with other vowel and consonant sounds to form different words. Using the 'wheel of letters' given below, try to make as many words as you can using the ng sound. After you have made the list, read these words aloud, paying attention to the ng sound.

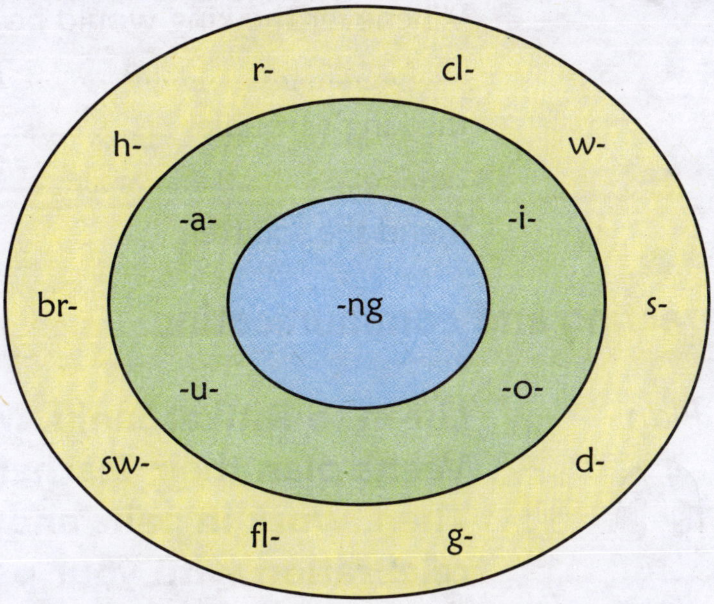

flung hung

D3. *Identify*

7.6

Listen carefully to this story and note down all the words that have the ng sound. Then, practise saying them aloud.

Dictation time

3 GOOD HEALTH AND WELL-BEING

E. *Listen and write*

DT

Listen and fill in the blanks.

Once there was a king. He had a .... for a friend. This squirrel ....! Whenever the king would be sad, he would .... The squirrel would listen to the king's troubles .... That would .... He was very proud of his friend the squirrel.

Interacting and communicating

Collaboration NEP

F1. *Plan*

7.7

Listen to Ritika, Sanju, Manu, Jyoti and Veena plan their Teacher's Day programme. Then, work in pairs and plan Teacher's Day celebration with your partner. Talk about the things you can do for your teachers.

F2. *Survey*

Go around the class. Ask your classmates which of the following activities do they want to do for Teacher's Day celebration. Write their names beside the activity they want to participate in.

Teacher's Day Programme

Card making: ....

Dance: ....

Group song: ....

Getting flowers: ....

Creativity · Collaboration NEP

F3. *Talk*

Imagine you are planning a birthday party for a friend. You need to arrange for games, songs, decorations and food. In groups of five, make preparations for the party. Tell each other what you can or cannot do.

Fun Activity

Some of us have pets. Think about the many ways you could take care of stray animals as well. For example, you can keep a clay saucer of water for the birds. Share your thoughts with the class.

8 How's the day today?

In this chapter, we will:

- listen for specific information.
- practise short conversations about the weather.
- learn to ask and answer questions about the type of weather we like.
- talk about our favourite leisure activity.
- learn to gather data and interpret it.

Getting started

A. *Mark* **Look at the pictures. Then, put a tick (✓) beside the happy face if you like the day and a tick (✓) beside the sad face if you don't.**

Windy

Cold

Sunny

Cloudy

Day	Like	Don't like
Windy	☺	☹
Cold	☺	☹
Cloudy	☺	☹
Sunny	☺	☹

Listening and learning

B1. *Listen* (8.1) **It is Monday morning. Ria and her friend Srijan are talking during lunch break about how they spent their Sunday. Listen to them.**

B2. *Sort* (8.2) **Listen to the conversation again. Here is a list of the things that Srijan and Ria did. What did Srijan do? What did Ria do? Write 'S' for Srijan and 'R' for Ria against each thing.**

1.	went for a picnic	☐	2.	read a storybook	☐
3.	played chess, carom	☐	4.	went swimming	☐
5.	helped mother in the kitchen	☐	6.	played cricket/football	☐
7.	watched television	☐	8.	went skating	☐
9.	went for a walk	☐	10.	went for dinner	☐
11.	slept early	☐	12.	arranged cupboard/ bookshelf	☐

B3. *Answer*

8.3

Surya went to Gangtok and Darjeeling this summer. Listen to Surya talk about his holiday. Then, answer the questions.

1. Which cities did Surya visit?

   ....

2. Gangtok is in which state?

   ....

3. How many days did Surya and family spend in Gangtok?

   ....

4. In which place did it rain heavily?

   ....

5. Which place is famous for a beautiful view of the sunrise?

   ....

6. What did they buy for their friends and relatives?

   ....

7. Which two temples did they visit?

   ....

8. How long was their holiday?

   ....

Speaking and practising

Collaboration • Communication Skills NEP

C1. *Ask and answer*

Read this conversation between Pranav and Pooja.

Manners matter!

When we are describing something, we use our hand movements to express our feelings. Hand gestures can be used to show that we feel strongly about something. We spread our hands to describe something big or raise them over our head to describe something tall.

Pranav: I don't like rainy days. They are so dull and boring!

Pooja: Oh, really? I love the rain! I make paper boats. I love watching them float in the rainwater. What days do you like?

Pranav: I love sunny days. They make me feel nice and happy.

Pooja: I love bright, clear days as well. But I don't like very hot days!

Now, form groups of four. Ask and answer questions about your favourite days.

C2. *Sort*

Go round the class. Find out from your classmates what their favourite leisure activity is. Make a list. Which activity is chosen by most people? Share the information with the class.

C3. *Share*

Tell the class what your favourite leisure activity is. Also, give reasons why you like it. Talk about it for one minute.

Word Wizard: Useful words and phrases

You can use these words while talking about leisure activities:

playing video games
bicycling
reading books
singing
drawing and colouring
playing football/cricket
watching television
dancing
skating
writing

Grammar Guide: Interesting language points

You may talk about your leisure activities in this way:

I like to .... because ....

For example,

I like to play football because it keeps me fit.

You may talk more about your leisure activity in this way:

Usually, my friends and I play in the nearby park. I quite enjoy it. If you want to play football, you'll require a football, a large field and at least five players.

Saying it right

Art Integration NEP

D1. *Sing* 8.4

Listen to this song and sing along.

One leaf—two leaves
How many does the plant have?
One calf—two calves
How many are there?
One knife—two knives
How many do we need?
One loaf—two loaves
How many do you want to eat?
One thief—two thieves
How many did the police catch?
One life—two lives
How many does the cat have?
Oh, so many, don't ask how many!

Info byte

Usually, when a word ends with '**f**' or '**fe**', we replace **f** or **fe** with '**ves**' to show its plural form.

life → lives

leaf → leaves

D2. *Repeat*

8.5

Listen to the plurals of these words and repeat them.

calf	–	calves
half	–	halves
elf	–	elves
hoof	–	hooves

knife	–	knives
scarf	–	scarves
loaf	–	loaves
dwarf	–	dwarves

Now, listen to the plurals of these words. Repeat them.

cliff	–	cliffs
proof	–	proofs
cuff	–	cuffs
puff	–	puffs

chef	–	chefs
bluff	–	bluffs
spoof	–	spoofs
roof	–	roofs

Did you notice the difference in the ending sound of these words?

D3. *Say aloud*

8.6

Now, listen carefully and write down the words in both their singular and plural forms. Then say aloud the words.

Singular	Plural

Dictation time

E. *Listen and write*

DT

Listen and fill in the blanks.

15 LIFE ON LAND

.... live in very cold climates. They have .... They also have a .... under their skin. That layer is called .... That keeps them warm. They sleep in .... They eat .... They are excellent ....

Interacting and communicating

F. *Survey* — **Go round the class. Ask ten of your friends about the type of weather they prefer. Which type of weather is preferred by most people? Put one tick (✓) for each person. Count the number of ticks and share the results with your class.**

Rainy	Cloudy	Cold	Hot	Sunny	Windy

Fun Activity

India Focus NEP

Some of us like to go to cooler places in summer. Here are the pictures of six famous hill stations in our country. Complete their names.

L .... KH

C .... RG

D .... R .... E E .... NG

.... H I .... L ....

O .... T ....

M .... N .... AR

9 It's playtime!

In this chapter, we will:

- learn to talk about simple everyday games.
- learn to talk about the rules of various sports and games.
- learn to match oral descriptions with images.
- learn the pronunciation of ch and y sounds.

Getting started

A. *Write*

Look at the picture below. Which game are the children playing?

1. The name of the game is:

    ....

2. Any one rule of the game is:

    ....

Listening and learning

B1. *Answer* 9.1

It's a free period in class. The children want to have fun. Mrs Sharma tells them about a game that they will all like playing. Listen to her explaining the rules of the game. Then, provide the following information.

1. Say what the 'actor' can/cannot do.

Can do	Cannot do

2. Say what the other team can do.

The other team can...

a. ....

b. ....

c. ....

3. The general rules of the game are:

a. ....

b. ....

c. ....

Word Wizard: Useful words and phrases

To describe the rules of a game, use words like 'can', 'cannot', 'allowed', 'not allowed', etc.

B2. *Listen* 9.2

Veena, Mayank, Mehmood and Mary are talking to each other about how they like to spend their Saturday evenings. Listen to them.

B3. *Match*

Look at the pictures of activities that Veena, Mayank, Mehmood and Mary like. Which activities are liked by whom? Write the name of the person below the picture. If an activity is liked by all of them, write 'All'. If no one likes an activity, write 'None'.

....

....

Speaking and practising

Communication Skills NEP

C1. *Tell*

Read the following conversation. Then, tell it to your friend using your own words.

Nikhil: Hi Neeraj, shall we play snakes and ladders?

Neeraj: Oh yes, do we have all we need?

Nikhil: Yes, of course. Here is the snakes and ladders board, and here are the dice, the dice cup, and the counters.

Dheeraj: Hi, may I join you? But I do not know how to play this game.

Neeraj: Oh, it's very simple. Do join us.

Nikhil: Here is how we play it. First, we place our counters on the space that says,'Start here'. We roll the dice. We take turns to do this.

Dheeraj: Okay.

Neeraj: We move the counters forward according to the number shown on the dice. If the counter lands at the bottom of the ladder, we move up to the top of the ladder.

Nikhil: And if the counter lands on the head of a snake, we slide down to the bottom of the snake. Whoever reaches the space that says 'Home' first is the winner!

Dheeraj: It's interesting, let's start!

C2. *Ask and answer*

Now, look at the picture of a game called 'Hopscotch'. How is this game played? Find out from your teacher. Make notes while your teacher explains the rules to you. Then, find a partner and take turns to ask and answer questions about hopscotch.

C3. *Say*

Look at these pictures. Do you like doing any of these activities? Say one sentence about each of them.

Word Wizard: Useful words and phrases

You can use the following words:

balloons	ball	sandcastle
seesaw	slide	monkey bar

Saying it right

Art Integration NEP

D1. *Sing*

9.3

Listen to the song and sing along.

A chicken with six chicks
Go cluck, cluck, cluck!
A cow with two calves
Go moo, moo, moo!
A pigeon and her squabs
Go coo, coo, coo!

A lion with its cubs,
A cat with its kitten,
A chipmunk with its pups,
A chimpanzee with its infant
Visit the zoo, to see them
play together!

D2. *Identify*

Look at the pictures. Say their names aloud. Which sound does each word begin with?

Now, practise saying these words aloud.

chain	chair	change
chalk	chimpanzee	chin
chocolate	chart	chest

D3. *Say aloud*

Look at the pictures. Then, say their names aloud. Which sound is common in these words?

Now, practise saying these words aloud.

yard	year	yes	yell
you	young	yeast	yet

Dictation time

Cross-curricular NEP

E. *Listen and write* DT

Listen and fill in the blanks.

.... is a martial art developed in .... There are .... belt colours. .... belt is for beginners. As you move from one level to the other, you get .... Karate is now popular all over the world. You may learn it as a sport or as ....

Interacting and communicating

Collaboration • Happiness Content NEP

F. *Play*

Do you know what this game is called? Do you know how it is played? Tell the class. Then, play this game in groups of four.

Fun Activity

Happiness Content NEP

What do you think may happen when a message is passed around in whispers? There is a popular game that is played this way. It is called Chinese Whispers.

Play the game in groups of eight students.

TAKE a break

Know Your Game

Form groups of five and surf the Internet to find out about the origin of one indoor and one outdoor game. Make a short presentation on any one of them, talking about:

- What is the game?
- What was it originally called?
- Do we have a similar game now?
- How was the game played then?
- How is it played now?

As a group, discuss how the games have changed and developed over the years. Fill in the timelines below to show the history of the game's development. At every vertical line, you have to write about the important developments or modifications done to the game. You may add more lines if needed.

Indoor game:

Outdoor game:

10 What's happening?

In this chapter, we will:

- learn to listen and talk about things that are happening at the present moment.
- learn to frame and answer questions in the present continuous tense.
- learn to frame meaningful sentences in the present continuous tense.
- learn to pronounce the two different sounds of th.

Getting started

A. *Complete* **Look at the pictures and complete the sentences.**

The boy is

....

The dog is

....

The girl is

....

The cat is

....

Listening and learning

B1. *Listen* 10.1

It is 7 o'clock in the morning. Kriti tells us what is happening at home. Listen to her.

B2. *Match* 10.2

Listen to Kriti's description again. Match the people with the actions. One person may be doing more than one thing.

5 GENDER EQUALITY

making dosas	wearing shoes
eating dosas	plucking flowers
washing the car	packing school bag
helping with making dosas	taking kids to school
watering the plants	cleaning up the dining table
arranging things in the prayer room	filling up the water bottles

B3. *List* (10.3)

Kriti wants her mother to tell her how she makes *aloo parathas*. Her mother tells her she must watch her making the *parathas* to learn better. So she's making them for dinner tonight. Listen to her describe the process of making *aloo parathas*.

What ingredients did Kriti's mother use to make *aloo parathas*? Make a list.

B4. *Choose*

Put a tick (✓) on all the actions that Kriti's mother performed while making the *parathas*.

frying
cooking
cutting
squeezing
chopping
slicing
mashing
kneading
boiling
adding
spreading
mixing
roasting

Speaking and practising

C1. *Describe*

Look around the class. Then, describe to your partner what any five of your classmates are doing.

C2. *Ask and answer*

Now read the lists below. List 1 has people or animals. List 2 has actions. Choose a partner. Ask and answer at least five questions with the help of the two lists.

List 1	List 2
The monkey	sleeping
My grandfather	climbing a tree
The bird	flying in the sky
My father	reading the newspaper
My teacher	playing football
My mother	watching TV
My brother	teaching grammar
My neighbour	running to catch the flies
My friend	ironing the clothes
The dog	studying for an exam

C3. *Describe*

It's a holiday today. Look at all the people enjoying themselves in a park. Describe what they are doing.

Word Wizard: Useful words and phrases

You can use the following words in your description:

playing	painting	selling	sitting	talking
walking	jogging	driving	running	kicking

Saying it right

Art Integration NEP

D1. *Sing* 10.4

Listen to this song and sing along.

Today is my birthday, I've turned nine.
Today's my day, oh it's mine!
'There you are then, my boy,' said Dad!
Thanks for your wishes, I'm so glad.
Come in the evening, it's a must,
Once all of you are here,
The cake will be cut!

D2. *Repeat* 10.5

Listen to the pronunciation of the words in the lists below. Then, repeat them. How are they different?

List A	List B
then	thin
that	thick
they	thank
there	thought
though	think

D3. *Read aloud*

Read the following sentences aloud. Underline all the th words. Use a blue pencil to circle the words where th is pronounced as in 'this' and a green pencil for words where th is pronounced as in 'think'.

1. There is a family of four. This is the father and that is the mother. Here is the sister, and there is the brother.
2. Three thieves thought of robbing a bank. They stole thousands of rupees from the bank in just 10 minutes before they were caught.
3. My best friend's birthday is on Thursday, the fifth of March. I haven't thought about what to get him yet!
4. Though the weather is rather cold, I feel very thirsty.
5. Rita's brother surprised her with 13 flowers for her thirteenth birthday party on the sixteenth of December.

D4. *Sort*

10.6

Listen to Tanmay and Tarun talk to each other during their visit to the zoo. Then, write the different words with the th sounds you hear in the correct columns. After that, read them aloud.

th as in *this*	*th* as in *think*

Dictation time

E. *Listen and write*

DT

Listen and fill in the blanks.

On ...., all of us at home are very busy. My mother .... My father .... with it. My brother and I ....

My grandfather and grandmother help us with it. In the evening, all of us .... by the tree and ....

Interacting and communicating

Collaboration • Communication Skills NEP

F. *Ask and answer*

Look at the picture of a train's compartment where people are doing different things. Work in groups of four and ask and answer questions about the picture.

Word Wizard: Useful words and phrases

You can use the following words:

bunk/berth	suitcase	travel	luggage
sleeping	sitting	talking	working

Fun Activity

Happiness Content • Art Integration NEP

Play this game with your friends. You will need a dice and counters.

Rules of the game:

1. Place the counters on the 'Start' cell. Roll the dice and move your counter according to the number on the dice.
2. Enact the action shown on that cell within 30 seconds.
3. If someone cannot enact the action, he/she passes it to the next player and misses the next turn.
4. The first person to reach 'Finish' wins.

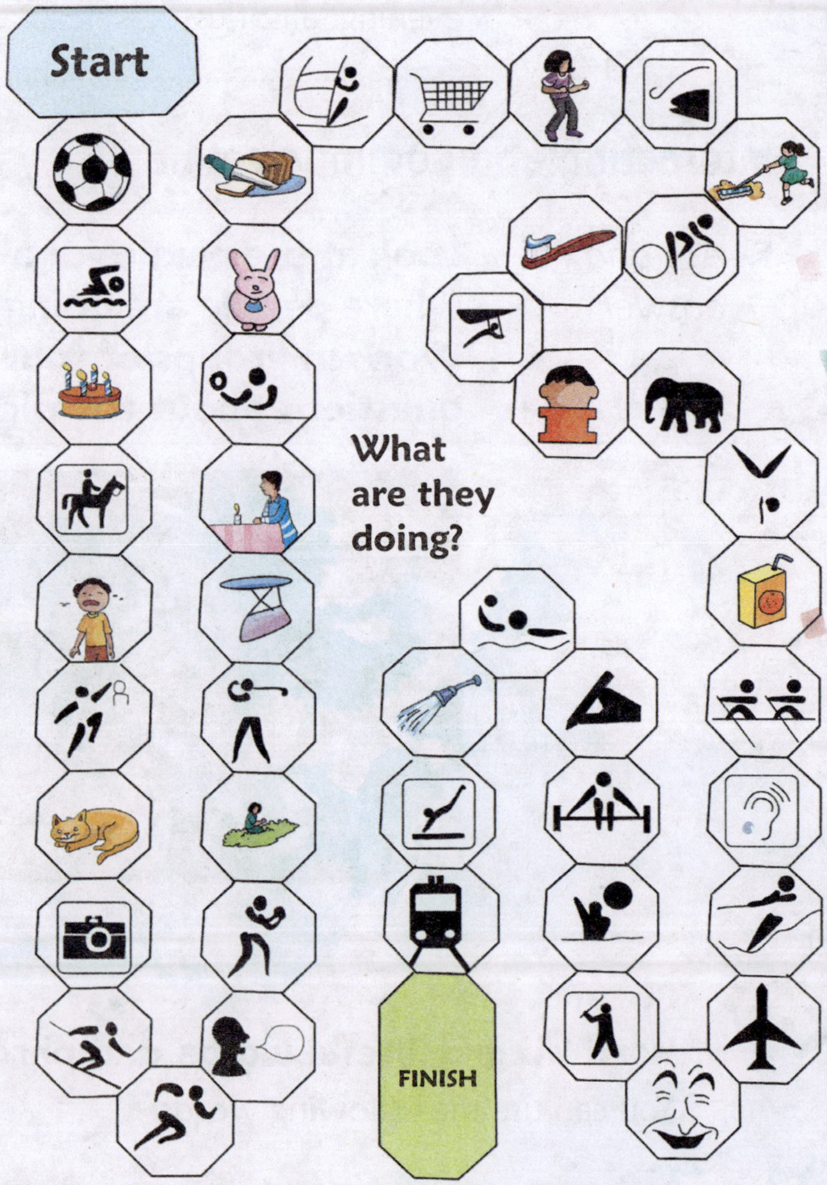

11 How will it be?

In this chapter, we will:

- listen to and learn the words used to plan a holiday.
- ask and answer questions using the simple future tense.
- learn to take quick decisions using the simple future tense.
- talk about planned events in the future.

Getting started

Cross-curricular NEP

A. *Talk* **This is a picture of how the weather will be in the following week. Talk about how any one day of the week will be like.**

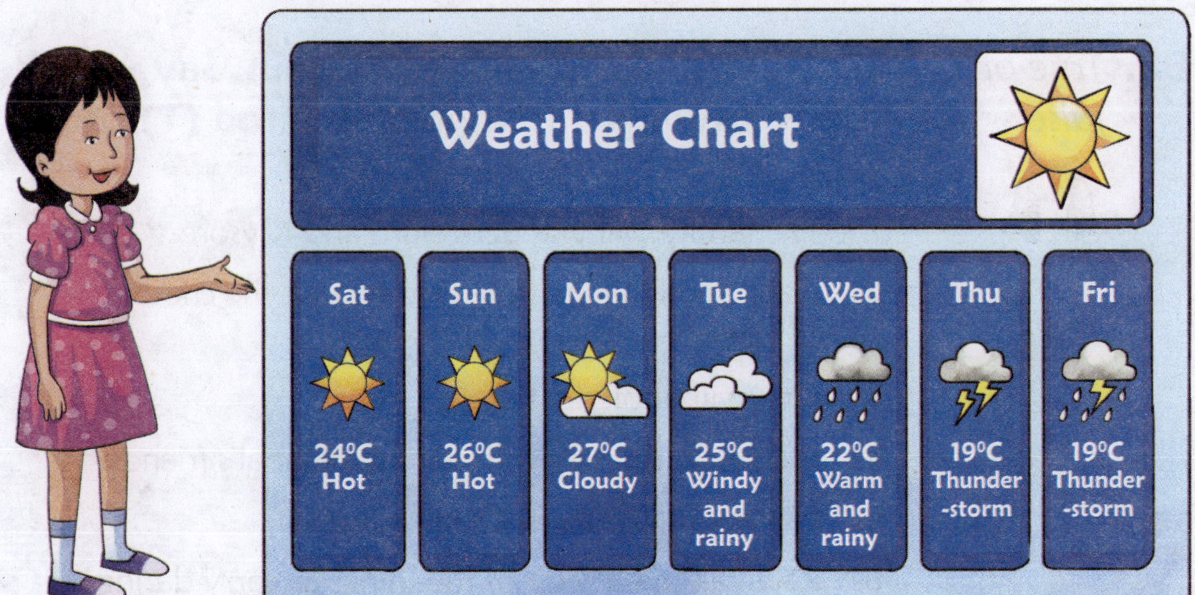

Listening and learning

B1. *Listen*

11.1

Renu is studying in Class 3 and her brother Ravi is in Class 5. They have just finished their exams. Now they will have holidays for two weeks. Their parents, Bina and Gopal, are planning a family vacation. Listen to the family discussing their holiday plans.

B2. *True or false*

11.2

Listen to the conversation again. Say whether the following statements are true (T) or false (F).

1. The family will visit Bengaluru and Mysore. ☐
2. Renu and Ravi are not happy about the choice of places. ☐
3. Bina will book the tickets. ☐
4. In Bengaluru, they will stay with Gopal's friends. ☐
5. In Mysore, they will stay in a hotel. ☐
6. Ravi will make a list of the things to carry during the trip. ☐
7. Renu will pack her bag herself. ☐
8. Gopal will select the places to visit in each city. ☐
9. The family will start preparations for their tour after two days. ☐

B3. *Answer*

11.3

Ten-year-old Sandra is doing her homework. Her mother is helping her with it, but she is also writing something. Sandra wants to know what her mother is writing. Listen to them talking.

Now, answer the following questions in a word or two.

1. What will Sandra's mother do on Monday?
2. When will she take Grandfather for an eye check-up?
3. When will she meet the dentist? Why?
4. What will she do on Thursday?
5. What will Sandra's mother get for her from the market?
6. What will happen on Friday?

Speaking and practising

Creativity • Collaboration NEP

C1. *Talk*

Look at this conversation.

Work in pairs. Think of five things that will happen or that you have to do in the future and tell your partner about them. You may first write the sentences in your notebook and then say them aloud.

Examples: There will be a parent–teacher meeting this Saturday.

We will have special assembly tomorrow.

Now, share your sentences with the class.

Grammar Guide: Interesting language points

To talk about an action that is yet to happen, we use the simple future tense.

We use 'will' with the action word to talk about actions in the future.

Examples:

We will go for a picnic this weekend.

I will meet you tomorrow evening.

Art Integration NEP

C2. *Role-play*

Read this conversation.

Vinod: Will you go to Susan's birthday party this evening?

Preetam: Yes, I will.

Vinod: Will you participate in the kite flying competition next week?

Preetam: Sorry, I won't be able to participate. I want to complete my project work.

Manners matter!

When you are making plans with others, listen to what they are saying. While speaking, don't raise your voice. Be polite. You must not sound like you are forcing your choice on others. If you cannot take part in something, give a reason why you cannot. It is polite to say 'thank you' when someone offers you an idea or a suggestion or 'sorry' when you cannot accept an invitation.

Imagine that your mother is asking you to do the following things.

1. Go with friends to the picnic next Saturday.
2. Watch a film on Sunday.
3. Go with daddy to meet your grandparents.
4. Participate in the fancy dress competition on Friday.
5. Bring friends home this evening.
6. Water the plants tomorrow.
7. Take the dog for a walk in the morning.
8. Clean your cupboard this Sunday.

Role-play the situations with your partner. One person will be the mother and the other will be the child.

C3. *Match*

Read the conversations given below. Then, match the statements in Column A with the quick decisions in Column B. Practise saying these with your partner.

Info byte

We can use **will** to talk about quick decisions and planned actions.

Mary: I'm hungry.

Sarah: I will make a sandwich for you.

Mary: That will be nice. Thank you!

Sarah: You are welcome.

Trisha: I have a sore throat.

Jatin: I'll make you some ginger tea.

Trisha: I'll like that. Thank you!

Jatin: You are welcome.

Column A	Column B
1. The fridge is empty.	a. I'll switch on the heater for you.
2. This sum is too difficult.	b. I'll call a taxi.
3. I'm in a hurry to go out.	c. I'll play with you.
4. I've lost my pencil.	d. I'll answer it.
5. The phone is ringing.	e. I'll help you solve it.
6. I'm too tired to walk.	f. I'll give you mine.
7. It's too cold in the room.	g. I'll help you pack your bag.
8. I'm bored.	h. I'll buy some vegetables.

Saying it right

Art Integration NEP

D1. *Sing* 11.4

Listen to this song and sing along.

There lived three sheep,
John, Jacob and Jobs.
They sailed in a big ship,
Dressed in sailor's robes.

D2. *Say aloud* 11.5

Listen to the words. Pay attention to the long or the short middle sound in each word. Then, say the words aloud.

fit	bit	sit	hit
lip	ship	tin	hip

feet	beat	seat	heat
leap	sheep	teen	heap

D3. *Sort*

Read the words aloud and write 'L' for the long middle sound and 'S' for the short middle sound in the box.

1. sing		2. sleep	
3. sip		4. tip	
5. whip		6. pin	
7. bean		8. beat	
9. kit		10. hip	
11. heap		12. keep	
13. bin		14. weep	

Dictation time

13 CLIMATE ACTION

E. *Listen and write*

Listen and fill in the blanks.

We all want to live in a .... planet. To achieve that, we must not burn .... We must not waste water. We must save electricity by .... of things like the .... We must not clear away forest lands. Instead, we should .... That will help us keep our planet clean and green for .... as well.

Interacting and communicating

India Focus • Collaboration NEP

F. *Discuss* **Work in pairs. Here is a two-day travel itinerary for tourists visiting Nagarjunasagar from Hyderabad. Tell your partner what the tourists will do on Day 1. Your partner will tell you what they will do on Day 2.**

Itinerary

Day 1

7:00 a.m.	–	Departure from Hyderabad to Nagarjunasagar by an AC bus
9:00 a.m.	–	Breakfast on the way
11:00 a.m.	–	Arrival at Nagarjunasagar Launch Station
11:30 a.m.	–	Visit Nagarguni Konda museum
12:00 p.m.	–	Depart to Srisailam by a boat
1:00 p.m.	–	Lunch on the boat
5:00 p.m.	–	Arrive at Srisailam
6:00 p.m.	–	Visit the temple
8:00 p.m.	–	Dinner and stay at a hotel

Day 2

8:00 a.m.	–	Breakfast at hotel
8:30–10.30 a.m.	–	Visit Ropeway and Pathala Ganga
10:30–11.30 a.m.	–	Visit tribal museum
12:00–1.00 p.m.	–	Shopping
1:00 p.m.	–	Lunch
2:00 p.m.	–	Departure for Farahabad
3:00 p.m.	–	Visit Farahabad Forest
4:00 p.m.	–	Departure for Hyderabd
9:00 p.m.	–	Arrival in Hyderabad

Fun Activity

Happiness Content • Art Integration NEP

Where would you like to go in your next vacation? Draw that place in the space given below. Show it to the class. Be as creative as you can be.

Saying it better!

Common mistakes	Use this instead
I'm *seeing* TV	I'm *watching* TV
I'm *watching* them.	I'm *looking at* them.
I'm *hearing* you.	I'm *listening to* you.
I can *listen* someone coming	I can *hear* someone coming.
I and my brother are both tall.	*My brother and I* are both tall.
Prema and me are good friends.	*Prema and I* are good friends.
She *tells* that she is hungry.	She *says* that she is hungry.
I *said* him I was coming.	I *told* him I was coming.

If you like the food that you are eating, don't simply say *it's nice*. You may use these words instead: *yummy, tasty, delicious, mouthwatering, heavenly, enjoyable*	If you are scared, don't simply say *I'm scared*. You may use these words instead: *tense, afraid, frightened, terrified, horrified, anxious*
If you are happy, don't simply say *I'm happy*. You may use these words instead: *delighted, excited, thrilled, glad, elated, overjoyed*	If you are hungry, don't simply say *I'm hungry*. You may use these words instead: *starved, famished, ravenous*

Common phrases

Common phrases to ask how someone is

- What's up?
- What's new?
- How are things with you today?

Common phrases to say how you are

- I'm doing great!
- Top class!
- Pretty good.
- Same as always.
- Not so great.

Common phrases to thank someone

- Thank you very much.
- I really appreciate it.
- I'm truly grateful.
- That's so kind of you.

Common phrases to respond to thank you

- My pleasure
- No worries
- No problem

Common phrases for agreeing

- Exactly
- Absolutely
- Seconded
- I agree with you completely.

Common phrases for disagreeing

- Not necessarily.
- I'm not so sure about that.
- Let us agree to disagree.

Common phrases to respond to good news.

- Awesome!
- How wonderful!
- That's great news!

Common phrases to respond to bad news.

- Oh no!
- That's terrible.
- I'm so sorry to hear that.

Common phrases for being tired

- I'm exhausted.
- I feel like lead.
- I can hardly keep my eyes open.

Children's Literary Fest

Did you know that *The Lion King* is one of the most popular children's films of all time? The original animated film was released in 1994. Recently, the film was remade in 2019. The animations were upgraded to make it seem real. The film was once again a superhit.

Watch the film either by yourself, or with friends or as a class.

A. **Sing Along**
The Lion King has many songs. Form groups and pick your favourite song from the film. Then, sing to the class as a group.

B. **Fashion Show**
You have to plan with your group beforehand. Dress up as characters from the film. Then, parade as a group for your class as they score you on your creativity, make up and originality.